Discover *the* real you!

Glow

10 step guide

DEDICATED TO

This book is dedicated to the memory of
Alex Latimer (14th Feb 1959 – 23rd Oct 2012)
and to all of the strong, courageous women
who rise above their circumstance to make a
difference and inspire others to GLOW.

GIVING LIFE OPPORTUNITIES TO WOMEN

GLOW © 2017 by Chara Clarke

Paperback   ISBN: 978-0-9934910-8-5

Permission granted
THE HOLY BIBLE, NEW INTERNATIONAL VERSION®, NIV® Copyright © 1973, 1978, 1984, 2011 by Biblica, Inc.® Used by permission. All rights reserved worldwide.

Published by
Maurice Wylie Media
Bethel Media House
Tobermore
Magherafelt
Northern Ireland
BT45 5SG (UK)

Publishers' statement: Due to the sensitivity of these stories some names and places have been changed to protect their identities.

For more information visit
www.MauriceWylieMedia.com

ENDORSEMENTS

"I am beyond proud of the GLOW team and Chara. Not only has Chara completed our Social Innovation Accelerator over the last six months, but at every step of our journey together, she has displayed a willingness to constantly learn, adapt, refine and challenge herself and the team beyond both the immediate problems and opportunities they have faced, in order to reach and realise the future possibilities. This means they live out the values and messages they encourage young women to explore in the GLOW programme. This book is but one of numerous examples of their tenacity and foresight.

It is fantastic to see their story being told and their resources and experience being shared.

So proud and honoured to be part of the journey so far and know this is just the beginning. Keep dreaming big, girls!"

Janene Ware,
Programme Manager for *The Young Foundation & Amplify NI* (Northern Ireland)

"Lighthouse first became aware of GLOW in 2015 and since this time has strived to source funding, to ensure we can avail of this course each year. From the initial course, which has been GLOW facilitated within Lighthouse a total of five times, we have found the course facilitators and managers, a pleasure to work with.

In terms of attendees we have had nothing but highly positive feedback from our service users. We have had the privilege of watching these women, many of whom were using Lighthouse services due to suicidal bereavement; anxiety and depression and/ or social isolation, flourish during their time within the group. One attendee spoke about how when she first joined the course she"... Felt like a closed-cup mushroom and by the end of it felt like a portobello."

This metaphor describes perfectly what the GLOW course was able to provide for so many attendees and how much self-confidence and social support they gained throughout the five-six weeks. In developing their own social support systems and networks and developing their own sense of self and worth, this course has had a hugely beneficial impact to the lives of many of those who attended.

It is our belief that this handbook will be of great benefit to women of all ages and circumstances and is a very positive extension and development on the amazing work already provided through GLOW. We hope to continue to use this course, for as long as it remains available, in the support and recovery of Lighthouse service users."

Sharon Quinn,
Lighthouse. www.LightHouseCharity.com

"GLOW is a programme that allows women to come together in a safe and confidential environment to share their life stories no matter what background or political beliefs they have. Everyone's voice is important and given an opportunity to be heard.

GLOW allows women to realise that 'bread and butter' issues are the same in all areas, women experience the same problems across all divides.

It builds confidence along with personal development goals, making it ideal for women who have never had time for themselves or been allowed or had the opportunity to take part in any programmes like GLOW.

The handbook is a great tool to encourage other women to take part in the programme. It tells stories of ordinary women and how hard life was for them.

It lets women see that they are not on their own and through the personal development of the programme they can lead stronger and happier lives.

There should be more programmes like GLOW delivered at grass roots level. Well done Chara!"

Una McRoberts,
Ardoyne/Shankill Health Partnership.

CONTENTS

ABOUT GLOW

It all began in 2008 with a small group of women who wanted to reach out into the community in a practical way. They held pamper nights and Christmas dinners for local women from all communities, connecting and building relationships while breaking down religious and social barriers that had stood for generations.

They discovered that no matter what community women come from, many face the same situations such as depression, anxiety, low self-esteem, financial difficulties, family issues and much more. In 2012 they delivered their first Personal Development Programme to help women build their confidence and set positive goals in life.

Since 2012, hundreds of women have come through the programmes and activities. They have introduced new programmes that help develop the individual and equip them with whatever they need to reach their potential.

Their heart is for every woman to believe she is valuable and created for a purpose. They are passionate to come alongside women and help them discover their ambitions, dreams and desires; to embark upon the life they were created for.

Many of those who have went through the programmes have found work or returned to work, qualified as life coaches, volunteered with local community groups, set up their own businesses and built positive lasting friendships.

"Face your fear
& Do it anyway"

Introduction

Well done on picking up this book to begin your journey of discovering *The Real You!* Don't get me wrong, I'm not telling you that by reading this book, life is going to be perfect and everything will be figured out. I'm sure you know that life unfortunately just isn't that easy.

I'm not one of those people who believe that if you think happy thoughts that the universe will make it happen. There is no formula or magic wand to discovering your true identity and living a life of full potential.

I'll be honest, it takes hard work and some days will be harder than others. However, I want this book to be your support, encourager, motivator and inspiration, so you can believe that you've been created for a purpose. I want you to know that you've potential and hopefully this knowledge will empower you on your journey of discovering your identity and purpose.

How many of you had dreams when you were younger? Perhaps about a job or a career you really wanted to pursue, a hobby or just to be happy and secure. How many of you are living that life you once dreamed of?

What has stopped you from going after what you once were passionate about?

Was it fear, negative thoughts, self-doubt or circumstances out of your control?

If you continue to allow the fear to hold you back then you will still be in the same place in five and ten years from now and can I ask; "Do you really want to be in the same place?"

As a wise friend always said to me;

"What's the worst that can happen?"

Don't let fear be responsible for you missing out on life's experiences and opportunities.

Many times in my life I have had to face a fear of what will people say about me, fear of failure, fear of looking stupid or being wrong.

I had a fear of leaving my job and going full-time with GLOW. But I know that if I hadn't just stepped out, I would not be sitting here now writing this book telling these wonderful stories.

I was working part-time as an administration assistant within a local playgroup. As much as I enjoyed my job, I never felt fulfilled and always knew there was so much more that I was here on this earth for... have you ever felt like that?

When I established GLOW as a charity in 2011, I was still working part-time and using my other time between being a mum and getting GLOW up and running.

I was running GLOW voluntarily for several years with small pots of funding to deliver Personal Development Programmes. As GLOW began to snowball with more and more women signing up it began to get too much both working part-time and running GLOW, as running GLOW was becoming a full-time role.

I knew there was so much more potential within GLOW and so many more women we could reach. I began to feel burned out. I needed to still work in my job but my heart and passion lay within GLOW, I realised the change these programmes were making to women's lives.

My husband, who is a firefighter, began to notice that I was feeling overwhelmed as we were out one day for coffee. I broke down as the pressure was too much. He asked me what I wanted to do and I told him I wanted to leave my job and run GLOW full-time but financially we couldn't do it and the funding within GLOW wasn't as secure. He told me if that's what I wanted to do, then I should go for it!

I had feared being truthful to my husband about leaving my job, I had feared leaving a secure job to go into something that wasn't guaranteed to pay me. I had feared GLOW would fail, ultimately making me a failure. I had feared the unknown. But as I stepped into my new season with some fear, I also knew that if I didn't take this opportunity I would stay stuck and wouldn't fulfil my full potential.

The meaning of fear[1] is:

'an unpleasant emotion or thought that you have when you are frightened or worried by something dangerous, painful, or bad that is happening or might happen.'

Cambridge dictionary

---

[1] Definition of "Fear" from the online Cambridge English Dictionary, © Cambridge University Press, https://dictionary.cambridge.org/dictionary/english/fear. Accessed 25th October 2017. Used by permission.

Or I like to explain 'FEAR'...

False Evidence Appearing Real.

The Fight or Flight response is a physiological response triggered when we feel a strong emotion like fear. Fear is the normal emotion to feel in response to a danger or threat. Fear also is connected to anxiety. The Fight or Flight response[2] enables us to react with appropriate actions: to run away, to fight, or sometimes freeze to be a less visible target. If you continue to live in this cycle of fear and irrational thinking then this can lead to anxiety and feelings of worthlessness.

Although you may not be able to control your emotions you can control how you are going to respond. Are you going to freeze, run away or face your fear and do it anyway?

The first is usually the hardest and maybe choosing to read this book and be active within the activities, brings a sense of fear in what you might discover. I want to encourage you to take action anyway!

You have been created for a purpose with fantastic qualities, gifts and strengths. Don't waste these blessings by giving into fear. Take this journey with me and the other women whose stories are featured throughout this book. *Discover The Real You,* then go out and make an impact on your world.

I may not know you or your circumstances, but I believe in you. I can't help but look at women and see their potential and worth. I have witnessed hundreds of women who were once filled with fear, living a life of worthlessness and anxiety, grow in confidence, believe in themselves and begin to take action towards their dreams and goals through our steps.

---

2   The Fight or Flight response, also called hyperarousal, was first described by Walter Bradford Cannon.

How This Book Works...

This book is your safe space to be creative, real, honest, inspirational and confident.

For many of us women, talking can be easy. We love to sit around and have chats over a cup of tea and dare I say; cake! It's actions that make the most difference. Unless you take action, you are not going to move from the spot you're sitting in, no matter how much we dream.

So you have a choice as you read this book, you can either keep it on the shelf after reading the nice inspirational stories, or you can take action by being proactive throughout this book.

This book will teach you ten powerful strategies that will empower you to take action and move into your true identity. Each session outlines a strategy with an activity for you to complete so you can begin to take action immediately.

I want to encourage you to use this book and the blank pages to fill it with big dreams, courageous actions, bold goals and inspiring truth. Some activities are more creative than others. You will need lots of coloured pencils, magazines, paper and anything else you can get your hands on to release your creative side. Feel free to share your creative pictures and designs on our website to inspire others. I'll let you know later how to do that.

Why do you need to write?

There are so many positive reasons why writing down your thoughts and goals are important. The most important reason for doing so within this book is to help bring focus and clarity. There are so many thoughts that go around our heads throughout the day, it's difficult to sort out the important ones from the not-so important. Writing down these thoughts can help you eliminate the negative and self-defeating ones. Another good reason is, when we take thoughts and goals from our head, put it on paper and read it back, it clarifies things and when you look back over these pages, you can see how far you have come. So, remember to write, read over, clarify, focus on what's important and take action.

Why this book?

This book would not be possible without the fabulous GLOW women who have taken part over the years in our programme, *The Real Me*. They have bravely chosen to share their stories within this book to encourage and inspire you as you work through your journey of discovery.

I could add so many more life changing stories within this book of women who have had not just thoughts of suicide but attempted it. Numerous others with anxiety and depression, dependant on alcohol and drugs, suffering self-harm, abusive relationships, worthlessness and loneliness. After taking part in our programme their success stories continue to challenge and encourage other women and bring hope that change can happen with direction and guidance.

Many of these women after taking action and getting onto the path of discovering their identity have went on to employment, setting up their own businesses, training in counselling, mentoring and life coaching, further education and volunteering and the same can happen for you.

I want you to be the writer of your story!

I have had so many women over the years from various parts of the world contact me to ask if we run this programme in their area. This book is a way of connecting women all around the world, to journey with one another as you share your stories and journey with each other through our network.

This book is your starting point to begin to discover your true identity, *The Real You*. Imagine what your life will be like once you are walking in your true identity! Imagine the people around you who you can positively impact and help them to begin their discovery journey.

I believe in you, and together lets GLOW and *Discover The Real You!*

Love, Chara x

GLOW

Discover The Real You!

Angie's Story...

Before GLOW I was sad, in a dark place, feeling scared and lonely. I'm very good at putting on a front and smiling and pretending like everything was alright but when I went home I was starting to scare myself because of some of the thoughts I was having and feeling so low.

I began to think that I needed to do something about what I was going through. Every day was getting worse so I knew I needed to reach out. I had a friend who had done *The Real Me* programme and I was curious as to what it was. I thought for a few days if I was really going to do anything about it and then decided; "Yes, I'm going to do this!"

So I added the page on Facebook and sent Chara a message about the opportunity to join the programme. For me, the thought of going into the sessions was absolutely horrendous and I had to talk myself round multiple times. The first morning, I had changed my mind several times about going, as I walked through the door to the centre, my heart was beating a mile a minute.

However, I soon learned that I had nothing to fear. GLOW actually makes you feel alive and it made my heart beat again. GLOW has saved my life, it has! It made me feel alive, gave me purpose to live and made me realise I'm a strong person and that I'm worth it. It's given me confidence and pushed me to boundaries I never thought I would go. It's empowered me to open up where I've hid things for 20 years of my life. It's given me the courage and strength to tell people that actually; "No, I'm not okay."

I loved the *'Stinking Thinking'* session. During my lowest days I would have thoughts I never really realised were 'stinking' and keeping me from moving forward. It helped me to be aware of my thoughts and when I would have certain thoughts it would trigger what I learned about *'Stinking Thinking.'*

In GLOW we all work as a group and we all feel like we could confide in each other, just listening to other people's stories really inspired me. There were two other girls in my group who have come through what I am going through and they have really encouraged me. I now feel there is light at the end of the tunnel.

The programme equips you with all the tools to help you in life but we were never pressured to talk or do an activity. It was just if you could do it - it is always up to you.

The confidence sessions were hard at the start, to think of things I had accomplished but then the other women were helping each other by naming different things we had all done as a group.

Another favourite session was *'I am Valuable'* - I was living my life how others wanted me to live with no real value or confidence in myself. This session equipped me to look at all areas in my life and discover that I actually have an important role to play in life, that I am valuable to my family and to myself and that I need to focus on myself and become the best me that I can in order to be the best person for others.

I have become a fighter, I am fighting to get my life back to the way I want it to be. I'm determined and the fire has been stoked again, the wind of purpose is on my back pushing me forward into life, my story isn't over yet.

You need to grow and find your confidence, do things you like to do, take time for yourself and do it for yourself!

"GLOW gave me back my life. My children have an energised mum full of confidence who's not afraid to cry, not afraid to say today's a tough one but tomorrow is a new day!"

Step 1

'I am valuable'

'Your value doesn't decrease based on someone's inability to see your worth!'

Unknown

Who am I?

What is my real identity?

Are these not questions every woman has asked herself at one point in her life?

Discovering *The Real You* is a journey, there will be ups and downs. So, no matter where you are on your journey, use this handbook to discover more about yourself.

Imagine a jug of water filled with six cups, each cup represents an area in your life that you pour into, give time and energy to.

Fill each cup up every time you give attention to that area. If you keep filling up the cups then what is left in the jug at the end?

That's right...It's empty.

So how can you give time and energy to these important areas in your life if you are running on empty?

You need to start realising that you are valuable and you need to be filled. You need time for yourself to build you up in order for you to be able to give your best to those who are important in your life.

First you need to get some perspective and focus in your life. You need to have a visual of the important areas in your life and recognise all that you do. This exercise will help you step outside of your daily living and open your eyes to a new perspective on areas in your life you give too much time to and areas you need to focus on more.

"GLOW gave me the chance to move on with my life and to get up in the mornings and go out more, rather than just sit in the house without getting dressed. I take chances and do things I wouldn't have dreamt of doing and now I just feel like a totally different person."

Task

Put a photo of yourself in the circle below. Around the circle, list all the titles and roles you play within your life. For example; mother, wife, care-giver, friend, boss, sister, budget manager, taxi driver, nurse.

HOW MANY CAN YOU THINK OF?

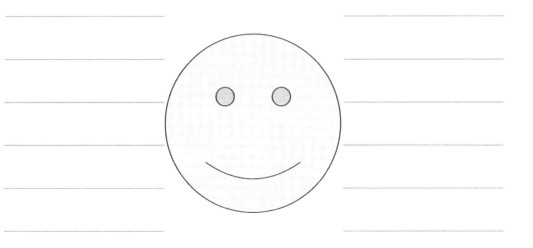

Use these pages to expand on every role of your life. List the roles, then write down all the qualities and strengths you bring to this role.

Do you feel fulfilled in this area?

Does it drain you or energise you?

Are you giving too much time to this role that could be time spent in another role?

Think about what roles you fill on a day-to-day basis. You will begin to see you do a lot more than you think!

Notes...

Elizabeth's Story...

I had an unloving childhood so to get away, I married young but I didn't realise I was going somewhere worse. My husband became abusive so I left after a number of years. I remarried and things were better, but in the end, he left for someone else after years of marriage.

Lonely, empty and angry, I tried not to show how I felt, so I wore a mask during the day but at night time was when I was most lonely and when I cried and reflected on how all this could happen.

I didn't want to burden those closest to me with my heartache and I think they avoided raising the subject as they obviously could see my hurt but this meant, I just kept it all to myself. I thought I was being really good at hiding my feelings but my daughter obviously saw what was really going on and is the one who had talked with Chara about the programme. I didn't have any choice, she just hit me with it one day and said; "We're going to see Chara and you will sign the papers and do whatever you are supposed to do!"

So I did what I was told! The first few weeks were a bit daunting but you realise everyone at the table has a story to tell. We were all crying at everyone else's stories, so you think to yourself; "I'm not alone."

You start to build friendships and really become one with each other. Everyone is a total stranger and you don't know what's going to happen.

When I started GLOW, I was in a low place with no confidence.

But before I knew it, I was getting up in the mornings and going out more, rather than just sitting in the house without getting dressed. Because of the programme, I now take chances and do things I wouldn't have dreamed of doing before and now I just feel like a totally different person!

I enjoyed all the steps but one that really grabbed me was the 'Glance Back' session.

I realised as people were sharing their stories, that others are also wearing a smile but could have something going on behind the mask. The session was like bringing me back to the bones but it was a really good thing to do. Everyone got to a point where they would just sit down and take deep breaths and let it all out and we all seemed to feel good afterwards.

You are quite busy thinking about yourself in your own misery, that you never think that anyone else has a story as bad as yours. I would think to myself that I'm actually quite lucky in some ways when I hear what others have been through. There are people who are going through worse battles and this was a learning experience for me. I think about others more than I did before, like strangers and older people.

Through the session 'I am Wonderfully Made' it empowered me to look at myself in a different perspective, that I am a human being whereas before I had no self-worth at all.

Even my daughter says I am getting back to that confident woman. I prefer this version of myself, I am happier in myself and happier when I am with others. Nobody can change their past but I have learned how to cope with what I have been through. I think if you are forgiving then it means you can get through anything. Once you forgive yourself, everything else just gets on with it.

Mental health is a really big issue but I'm not ashamed and you don't have to feel ashamed either. I would recommend every woman to try GLOW, it has really changed my outlook on life. It is really good for anyone suffering hard times or for those who feel stuck and just want to move forward.

"*You're quite busy thinking about yourself in your own misery, that you never think that anyone else has a story as bad as yours. I would think to myself that I'm actually quite lucky in some ways when I hear what others have been through. There are people who are going through worse battles and this was a learning experience for me. I think about others more than I did before, like strangers and older people.*"

Step 2

'I am wonderfully made'

> *'True beauty in a woman is reflected in her soul.'*
>
> Audrey Hepburn

The meaning of 'Self-awareness' is:

'Good knowledge and judgement about yourself.'

Self-awareness empowers your journey of self-discovery, enabling you to step away and examine the way you see and treat yourself.

Self-awareness is having an understanding of your personality, values, beliefs, thoughts and how to handle emotions etc.

Being aware of all this will help you to reach your full potential in life. As you become more self-aware you become better equipped to change how you think, ultimately changing how you act.

So we need to become more self-aware in order to change our thinking and actions.

Self-awareness is about knowing and understanding:

- Your beliefs and principles.

- Your own emotions.

- What motivates you.

- Your thinking patterns.

- Why you react to certain situations.

- What you want out of life.

You must become aware of your thoughts as this is the beginning of change and taking control of your future.

 DID YOU KNOW?

Your brain is actually more active when you are asleep! You think all day long and then at night when you are asleep, your mind is sorting out your thoughts.

As these thoughts are being processed, you are making choices and this creates proteins in your brain. So whatever you have been thinking about all day long, these are the thoughts your mind will sort out when you're asleep. These proteins will then turn to long-term thoughts.

These self-awareness questions will begin to help you think and focus on who you really are and maybe prompt some life changing actions.

It all starts with a thought...

"Watch your thoughts,
they become words.

Watch your words,
they become actions.

Watch your actions,
they become habits.

Watch your habits,
they become your character.

Watch your character,
for it becomes your destiny."

Chinese proverb

Author unknown

Self-Awareness Questions...

1. What have been your happiest moments in life and why?

2. What would you do, if you could do any job in the world and why?

_____

_____

_____

_____

3. What do you hope to achieve most in your life? (Think about what theme you would like your life to be, what are the areas you are most passionate about in life?)

_____

_____

_____

_____

4. What's your pet hate?

5. What relaxes you?

_____

_____

_____

_____

6. What gets you angry? (A passionate anger that makes you want to do something, to make a change.)

_____

_____

_____

_____

7. What do you truly value in your life?

8. What stresses you out, stops you from pursuing things or getting anything done?

Now what?

Now you are more aware of areas in your life you possibly have never thought about, or never had the chance to change. This is the time you can do something about it. Once you are more self-aware in some areas in your life, you will begin to recognise other areas you will become more aware of.

You can now use this information to make changes in your life, to stop being frustrated about things you think you cannot change.

Start making the positive choices in your life and eliminating the things that are holding you back.

There will be some areas in your life you can change, other areas that will take time and some areas that are out of your control. But this self-awareness will empower you to know how to handle these situations better.

> *"Whether you think you can,*
> *or you think you can't - you're right!"*
> Henry Ford

What actions are you taking to make any of these things happen? What areas do you need to change or focus more on?

Notes...

Tasleem's Story...

22nd April 2012 was the day my life changed forever. My beloved husband of nine years, at the age of 34, went out to work and tragically died. We had two sons aged six and eight at the time. Our family was completely broken, my kids were devastated and I was left afraid and alone.

I am originally from Pakistan and I moved to Belfast when I married my husband. He was a business owner and worked very hard providing for myself and our children. My husband took care of everything and I was happy as a stay at home mum looking after the children. I had never worked and had no real skills that I thought mattered.

So when my husband died suddenly, you can imagine how afraid I was. My family were all in Pakistan, I felt so lonely and had a sense of hopelessness. I was afraid, for myself and my kids, of going hungry, becoming homeless and for our future. The following weeks were hell, I was in such a dark place and could see no way out of this despair. I was grieving so much for my husband and my children were grieving for their father who they absolutely adored.

I knew Chara to say hello to as our two boys were in the same class at school. When Chara found out about my husband, her and one of the other mums at the school, Alison, reached out to support me at this time. Chara told me about GLOW and suggested I came on the programme to meet other women and see how it could help me move forward with my life.

At this point when I began the GLOW programme I remember

hearing other women's stories and my heart went out to them, I thought there is so much hurt and brokenness, we need to support one another. I suddenly began to feel not so alone, I knew I had support.

As my husband was the one who provided the finances and paid the bills I didn't even know where to begin. This is when I started to receive more support from Chara and GLOW. I had no income and I remember one of the lowest points was when my son was crying to my friend saying; "Mummy has no money to feed us today." I knew I needed to take control of my situation, that there was no one else who was going to look after and provide for my children, only me.

I asked Chara to help me with my benefits as I had no clue where to even begin. We contacted Tax Credits and they asked me for my National Insurance Number and I didn't even know what that was. I had to start from the basics. My husband and my children were all British citizens but I wasn't. Chara supported me through this difficult time and I began to get up on my feet.

The GLOW programme was helping to build confidence and self-esteem within me. I knew I wanted my children to have the best life possible as my husband would have wanted the same, so I knew staying on benefits wasn't an option, but I had never worked a day in my life and I didn't know what I could work at, especially with two young sons.

One day Chara asked me what I was good at and I said threading eyebrows, so she encouraged me to start with that. So with one small spool of thread I found in my sewing kit, I began to thread eyebrows for a small fee in my front living room.

That was four years ago. Today I have a separate studio in my home, I have set up my own business. I have been able to pay for over 11 training courses to learn new skills for my beauty business such as brows, lashes, nails, make-up, spray tan and so much more. I have been able to afford to visit my family in Pakistan three times, I have bought my own car and refurbished my whole house.

I am so proud of myself and feel so much more confident and happy that I am providing for my children. My sons have said that they have a happy mummy now and my parents and close friends are so proud of how far I have come.

GLOW helped me recognise that I needed to get rid of the negativity and surround myself with positive people who would support my dream and believe in me. I discovered that my future was in my control and I had to choose to do something about it, take action and be brave to make changes.

I didn't want to get to 90 years old and look back in regret and misery. If I did not take control now then nothing would change for me and my children.

My business is growing and I'm loving what I do. I tell people all the time; "Don't give up, follow your dream and even if you fall down, get back up and aim towards your destiny."

When I was asked what I think my life would have been like, had I not taken part in GLOW, I said; "I don't even want to imagine it!"

GLOW saved my life, being part of a group who support one another and where staff go that extra mile to help in whatever way they can, I can't thank them enough and my children thank them too.

Step 3

'To become
wise obtain
WISDOM'

'Do not forsake wisdom, and
she will protect you; love her,
and she will watch over you.'

Proverbs 4v6 NIV

Sorry for being a bit morbid, but did you know the number one regret most people have is that they did not live a life that was true to them but lived how others expected them to live?

Imagine yourself at 90. What would your 90-year-old self say to you now? With many more years of life, experience and wisdom, what expert advice do you think she would say?

Task

Write a letter to yourself with advice from that wise old 90-year-old woman.

Tip: Be realistic, don't tell yourself what you think someone else would say, only you know what is best for you and with more wisdom, your own advice will be more valuable than any self-help book.

Maxine's Story...

When I took part in *The Real Me* programme with GLOW, I was at the lowest point in my life. My marriage of over two decades had ended and my life as I had known it was over. I was broken, lost, hurt and fragile. *The Real Me* programme could not have come at a more significant time for me. I was at rock bottom and so for the first couple of sessions all I did was cry as I felt so raw. Each session revealed something new about myself that I hadn't recognised before or had just forgotten.

One of those learnings was that I can't change the past but I can take control of my future. I rediscovered my personal strengths and values that enabled me to look to the future with hope and self-belief. I began to embrace who I was and what I was capable of overcoming. I didn't want to stay stuck in the past feeling vulnerable and hurt. I wanted to move forward and embrace all that I could be. Yes my life would be different, but it didn't have to be a bad different. There's adventure to have, friends to make and fun to enjoy. Life began to take a positive turn as I could now see light at the end of the tunnel.

Another significant turning point during the programme was the *'Stinking Thinking'* session. I discovered it was so easy to fall into negative thinking, most of the time we don't even realise we're thinking negatively. Should it be about ourselves, our situation or about others. This negative mindset can hold you back and keep you in a dark, worthless situation. Through this session, I learned great skills on how to get rid of the negative thoughts and focus on positive thoughts. I was amazed at how quickly my mood lifted as I recognised I had the control to change my thoughts and moods. This change positively effected my home life with my daughters as they began to see a more happier, confident mum.

Since completing *The Real Me* programme, I am constantly referring women to take part. I have met many women who have similar circumstances to myself, I can show them that there is light at the end of the tunnel. There is support and there are ways to overcome the raw, negative feelings that we think will never pass. I have been there, I remember how it felt but I am now out the other side embracing my new life with confidence and fulfilment.

I am happy to have become a mentor within GLOW to help other women become more confident and build their self-esteem, as well as supporting the programmes working with young girls. I am also on the committee of GLOW and I am so happy to be able to give something back to the community and empower other women to discover their true identity and purpose. As a wise woman always told me; "Onwards and Upwards." This wise woman was my wee mummy. I have now made this my life motto and I encourage myself and others with it. No matter what we face in life, we can always with the support of those around us get back up and keep moving forward. This programme was a life changer! I also need to express my gratitude to all my true, loyal friends who supported me and still continue to do so. I am so blessed to have them as part of my journey.

"GLOW made me look at myself in a different perspective, that I am a human being, whereas before I felt I had no self-worth at all!"

Step 4

'Stinking Thinking'

'Tell the negative committee that meets inside your head to sit down and shut up!'

Ann Bradford

The meaning of 'Stinking Thinking' is:

'A bad way of thinking, that makes you believe, you will fail, that bad things will happen to you, or that you are not a very good person[3].'

Cambridge Dictionary

Do you know someone who is constantly talking negatively, you feel drained after talking to them for even the shortest length of time, and if you admit it, you even try to avoid them! *Stinking Thinking* is a cause of low self-esteem and I'm sure it is very draining and tiring.

Every thought has an emotion attached to it. Whether it's a negative or positive thought. Do you ever hear a song or smell something and it brings back a memory from a long time ago?

A thought may seem like something that is fleeting. A thought may seem harmless and of no consequence. Often, we think of actions as having more impact than thoughts but actions are generated from thoughts.

If you are worrying about something that has popped into your mind, the more attention you pay to the thought, the more it will grow and develop. It can cause you to worry, affecting your concentration during the day, your sleep at night, even making you feel ill in the process.

---

3   Definition of "Stinking thinking" from the online Cambridge English Dictionary, © Cambridge University Press, https://dictionary.cambridge.org/dictionary/english/stinking thinking. Accessed 25th October 2017. Used by permission.

Changing your thinking pattern is essential to overcoming negative thinking. Consciously controlling your thought life means not letting thoughts rampage through your mind. It means learning to engage interactively with every single thought that you have, and to analyse it before you decide either to accept or reject it.

So let's look at some of these 'Stinking Thinking' patterns…

Common 'Stinking Thinking' Distortions

1. All or nothing – Everything is either all positive or all negative. There is never any in-between.

2. Over-exaggerating – You tend to view a single negative thing as an eternal pattern of negativity. If one bad thing happens, the world is obviously out to get you personally.

3. Rejecting the positive – You can't accept anything positive ever happening. So if something good happens, you always find a way to turn it into a negative or explain why it was a fluke.

4. Irrational thinking – You become a mind reader. You don't think rationally about the situation before jumping to conclusions and interpreting the situation to your own negative way without evidence to support your outcome.

5. Emotional reasoning – You assume that your negative emotions and feelings reflect actual reality. If you feel bad – everything is bad.

6. Personalisation – You take things personally and become very defensive at even the slightest perceived criticism.

Think of ways to overcome negative thinking.

Become aware of Stinking Thinking

TIP: Keep a record of what triggers your negative thinking, what thought or action can you do differently to make you feel and think differently?

What is the thought?

_____

How does it make you feel?

_____

What were you doing/who where you with that triggered this thought?

_____

What can you do differently or think differently?

_____

How does this make you feel now?

_____

Notes...

"GLOW works, it actually does make you feel alive and it made my heart beat again.
GLOW has saved my life, it has! It gave me the purpose to live and made me realise that I'm a strong person and that I'm worth it! It's given me confidence and pushed me to boundaries I never thought I would go. It's made me open up where I've hid for 20 years of my life. It's given me the courage and steps to tell people that I'm not okay."

Now you are well on your journey to discovering the Real You.

This next part will help you to build your confidence, self-esteem and set positive life goals.

Tricia's Story...

One day in 2017, I was volunteering in the local food bank. A friend who volunteered alongside me said; "Don't you get fed up pretending?"

I was shocked and I asked her; "Pretending what?"

"Pretending that you're okay, that you're happy." She replied. I couldn't believe what she was saying. I felt the tears prick my eyes. It stung as I had never actually taken the time to stop and really look at how I was coping with life. I just got on with it as most of us women do.

She continued; "Tricia, you're pretending that you are coping with issues when really inside you're far from coping. You aren't coping and if you don't get the help you need you could end up hitting a brick wall and worse case scenario a breakdown, but you think you've to stay strong for your kids and carry on pretending."

She gave me a hug as she could see that I was beginning to take in and finally see what others could see.

"I know the perfect thing for you, you should go to GLOW." She said. She pointed me in the right direction to meet up with Chara and get signed up. I sort of agreed but I wondered; "How is that going to help me?" I figured I had nothing to lose and everything to gain so I went that day and signed up.

I remember sitting there filling in the form and thinking what was I even doing? I already had been to counselling, it was good but still left me with the same issues as before. Still broken. But I was determined to give something new a try.

My first day at taking part in *The Real Me* programme we sat as a small group of women on the sofas drinking tea, chatting to girls I had never met before. I chatted away and even shared advice to one woman who was going through similar circumstances as I was. I suddenly realised, here I was again, putting on the same front as before. Look at me, happy, smiling Tricia with my make-up and hair done but inside that's not who I was, that's not how I was feeling. If you could look inside, you would see years of issues that had robbed me of any self-worth, confidence, love and friendships.

The Real Me programme began with introductions, telling everyone a bit about why we were there and what we wanted to achieve from the programme. Suddenly I began to cry and my mask slowly slipped off as I was sitting there feeling raw and vulnerable but in the strangest way, I felt protected and comfortable. How strange was that?

A new place, new people and yet I opened up and told them more than I had ever told anyone before. The Programme facilitator, Gemma helped to change my whole way of thinking about myself and about life. Every Monday and Friday were emotional days talking about how we see ourselves. Many of the tools and techniques showed us how to change the *'Stinking Thinking'* to positive thinking. We were also taught how to learn from our past experiences but to leave it there because we can't change our past – it happened. But what we can change is our future and to make it a brighter, better place.

All the women who took part in the programme were all struggling with issues, everything from domestic violence, abuse, low self-esteem, low confidence, negative thinking and loads more. We realised we had one thing in common though, we are all survivors who don't want to be known as victims, we want to be heroines winning battles!

GLOW helped me realise that I had unresolved issues that needed dealt with before I could move on and achieve more in life, which I did. I felt stuck, my past issues had created a negative mindset that was holding me back. The *Esteemable Actions* session showed me that I needed to begin to focus on tasks that will build my self-esteem and help me take positive actions towards goals that I have set.

Before the programme I never believed I deserved to be happy but this session helped me to take back control and build my self-esteem and self-worth.

I can hand on heart say without GLOW, *The Real Me* programme and the constant support from Gemma, Chara and the GLOW girls, I would never have had the confidence to move forward in life, as I was stuck.

Now in case you are reading this thinking; "Jeez, that all sounds very sad." Let me reassure you that we had many laughs too. Sometimes more than we should.

Anyway, remember the girl at the top of this story, the pretender? Well she is gone and good riddance to her! She has been replaced with a lighter heart and mind, she has been turned into a confident glow-getter who wants to inspire others who are in the same position she was pre-GLOW!

I began my first year at college in 2017 to train in counselling, I began Health & Social Care with the local women's centre, and I have trained as a GLOW mentor to support women who are coming through the GLOW programmes. I have a craving for learning now, anything to equip me to better help other women with mental health issues become happier more fulfilled women, I'm there! See, even at the age of 43, it's not too late to follow your dreams.

GLOW gave me back my life. My children have an energised mum, full of confidence that's not afraid to cry, not afraid to say; Today's a tough one but tomorrow is a new day!" My family and friends have noticed a new Tricia too, though I have been warned that if I point out their *'Stinking Thinking'* one more time, I might get disowned!

*"Mental health is really a big issue
but I'm not ashamed and
you don't have to feel ashamed either!"*

Step 5

'Esteem-able Actions'

> *'Low self-esteem is like driving through life with your handbrake on!'*
>
> Maxwell Maltz

The meaning of 'Self-esteem' is:

'How well we value ourselves and how valuable we believe we are to the world. '

Cambridge Dictionary

Someone with positive self-esteem will generally approach things thinking they matter and have got something to offer the world.

If you have low self-esteem you may feel:

- Like you hate or dislike yourself.

- Worthless or not good enough.

- Unable to make decisions or assert yourself.

- Believe that no one likes you & become paranoid.

- You blame yourself for things that aren't your fault.

- Guilt for spending time or money on yourself.

- Unable to recognise your strengths and qualities.

- Feel you don't deserve happiness.

- Low in confidence.

Having good Self-esteem is important because it heavily influences your choices and decisions. In other words, self-esteem serves a motivational function by making it more or less likely that you will take care of yourself and explore your full potential.

Having low self-esteem can hinder you from living a purpose-filled, happy life.

Self-esteem can be developed from doing esteem-able actions for yourself and for others. Life should not be all about what we can get for ourselves, it's about recognising our giftings in order to help others, which builds confidence and self-esteem in others as well as ourselves. The truth is, it's our actions that guide and dictate our outcome. It's about the actions we take – the esteem-able actions that enable us to truly move out of the dark, negative thoughts and feelings and into the positive *Real You*.

Each day you'll be inspired to take on an Esteem-able Action that will move you past your limitations to a place you've likely never known. Each daily inspiration will be a baby step moving you closer to being the *Real You*. Often people say self-esteem is only about how you feel about yourself but the true self esteem is not only how you treat yourself, but how you treat each other.

Task 1

List 10 things you are proud of in your life. (Just start with one if that's all you can do.)

1 _____

2 _____

3 _____

4 _____

5 _____

6 _____

7 _____

8 _____

9 _____

10 _____

Task 2

We all have people or things in our life we can be grateful for, e.g. family, house, water, nature. It might be something small but when you think about how much you have to be grateful for, you recognise you have so much to live for.

Write a gratitude list.

I am grateful for…

Task 3

Acknowledge your positive qualities and things you are good at and avoid negative self-talk.

I am good at…

Task 4

Connect with people who love and care for you and treat you the way you should be treated. List these people and what you can do together.

Task 5

Nurture yourself at least once a day - do something nice for yourself. Make a list of things you will do for yourself each day.

Task 6

Set a challenge that you can realistically achieve, start with something small.

(One of our women stated that going to a coffee shop by herself was a huge step but something she really wanted to accomplish. This then led to her taking part in other activities and building new relationships.)

Task 7

Take regular exercise and eat a healthy diet. Physical activities are good for mental well-being. It will not only improve your self-image but will help with confidence and mental well-being.

List what you are planning to do:

Notes...

Rachel's Story...

The week before my wedding, my uncle died of cancer. With getting married, I didn't have time to grieve for him. Straight after getting married, I fell pregnant and had a really bad pregnancy. I had Hyperemesis Gravidarum, so was sick constantly, it was really draining. It lasted from 13 weeks right through to the birth. I was in and out of hospital on drips etc. It was an awful time.

After my son was born, I suffered two miscarriages. They were really hard for me. Both happened at 11 weeks gestation. Eventually I became pregnant again but thankfully this time I didn't miscarry. The pregnancy again, was very difficult. At just six weeks, the sickness began and I was soon diagnosed with Hyperemesis Gravidarum again. It was a hard pregnancy, I was constantly being sick until my son was delivered.

Just after he was born, my granny died. She had been suffering with dementia. It was just shortly after her death that things started to really get on top of me. I was really low.

When my youngest son was only six months old, I was diagnosed with post-natal depression. I was in a very low place. I stopped going out, I didn't want to do anything. I didn't wash, didn't get dressed. I lost all my confidence.

Then my friend Maxine, had come through *The Real Me* programme. I knew others that had done it so she suggested it to me. By this stage my son was three. I did listen to her but it took me a long time to think about doing it. Even finding out about the course was a real struggle for me. I kept putting it off. I just didn't want to think about anything. My mum and my husband started pushing me towards it, they wanted me to go and try it.

I reluctantly contacted Chara, she was lovely. She asked me to come down to the centre for a chat. This was already pushing me out of my comfort-zone as before this I had stopped going out, I had stopped driving. I was just so scared to go anywhere or do anything. I had a real fear of leaving the house in case I was killed or someone was killed. It was awful.

My mum agreed to drive me down to the centre, I went inside and spoke to Chara. She was lovely. I was petrified the whole way down in the car. I was so nervous, I was shaking but when I came in, she put me at ease.

Chara told me a little bit about the course and I signed up. It was a huge step for me. I couldn't quite believe I had done it.

A few weeks later, I was to start GLOW. I arrived the first day by myself. This was the first day I had driven anywhere in years. It was quite an achievement by itself. I only lived a few miles away but I might as well have been driving to Australia! It was so scary but I did it! I set this as my aim every week, this would be my motivation to leave the house, I would drive myself there and back every week for GLOW.

When I started the GLOW course, I really enjoyed the different steps. It was just everything that I needed to hear. My personal turning point was the week we went to the Belfast Activity Centre to do outdoor pursuits and team building activities. For me, even going on a trip was a massive task. Travelling in someone else's minibus, having no control was very hard but I did it. When we arrived, everyone was so encouraging so I actually ended up using the climbing wall which I never thought I would even attempt. I was determined though and I got to the top of it. Standing at the top of that wall, I actually started to question myself; "why am I so scared of everything?" I realised then, that if I could climb that, then I could do other things.

We were then encouraged to do the 'leap of faith.' This is where we climbed to the top of a 60ft pole then jump into nothing. Obviously we were wearing harnesses but it was really scary. The other girls below were cheering and shouting at me; "Come on Rachel, you can do this!" When I was able to do the jump, it really gave me confidence in other areas of my life.

After this, I started slowly by setting myself goals. I drove further distances in the car, I went out more etc. My confidence was growing daily. GLOW really changed my whole outlook on life. I was able to set up a parent/toddler group in my church. Something I never would have dreamed of doing before. I would highly recommend doing this, it has changed my life!

Step 6

'A confident woman'

'Optimism is the faith that leads to achievement. Nothing can be done without hope and confidence.'

Helen Keller

The meaning of 'Self-confident' is:

'Behaving calmly because you have
no doubts about your ability or knowledge.'

Cambridge Dictionary

Q: What does a confident woman look like?

Task

Using coloured pens, draw a silhouette of a woman, think of words or descriptions of what a confident woman would look like and act like.

Draw your silhouette woman

Think of someone you would consider to be confident and list
their qualities.

Confidence is:

- A state of being certain that a chosen course of action is the best or most effective.

- Having belief in your ability to succeed.

- To be self-confident is to be secure in yourself and your abilities.

- Confidence is the term we use to describe how we feel about our ability to perform roles, functions and tasks.

Think of areas in your life you are confident in.

- What makes you confident in that area?

- How did you become confident in this area?

- How can you use that confidence in other areas of your life?

Kate's Story...

As a young child I suffered an ongoing traumatic experience and this became a huge obstacle throughout my life. I never understood why this happened to me and through time the effects began to play a big part in my life. I always felt different and inwardly I constantly felt that I was a burden even though I wasn't. It affected me so much, in all areas of my life that I literally felt like I was just existing. There was so much pain and confusion, never having the courage to tell anyone what had happened. This continued for years, having no self-confidence or self-worth. Having trust in no one, never feeling secure and the only thing that saved me was to go into a 'bubble' as I called it. This was my safe haven, my protection. This had negative effects in the long run because I was never living in reality but it was the only way I knew, it was my survival.

Relationships with boys were really tough because I never felt I was good enough, I never trusted that anyone wanted me for me. At the age of eighteen I was in a deep relationship with my first real love. It was only through being with him that eventually I disclosed that I had suffered abuse and the effects of it for years. A few months later he passed away due to illness. This became additional trauma to everything else. A few years later I met my husband but had not dealt with a lot of the trauma and when I gave birth to my first child, everything came to the fore. I started counselling for a while but I'm not sure if it was the right time. For years I have tried to cope the best I can, I have always tried my best to be strong as I am so aware that my family depend on me.

I went to counselling two years ago and it was the counsellor that led me to GLOW. It was the lifeline that I needed in order to find myself, as I didn't really know who I was. Many times I had tried to stand tall against things that I felt were not right, but was usually put down and referred to as the one who had the problem. This caused so much damage that it just ate away at my self-worth and confidence. GLOW taught me that as much as I am a mother, wife, daughter, friend etc. I'm an individual too and that self-care is a must, regardless of the person or situation.

GLOW constantly reinforcing self-worth was such a big one for me. When you are told that you are 'this and that' everything is about you and nobody else's feelings count. You subconsciously go within yourself and don't take the time to respect your own feelings and values. GLOW has given me so much insight into myself and so many life skills to use. It's been an amazing experience and one that I would wish for every woman at some stage. I know that there will always be tough times in life, but hopefully now I can manage them a bit better. It comes down to positive mindset and self-care. I have found this programme has helped me so much, it's been life-changing.

'I am Strong' sessions helped me to recognise my strengths and discover how I can use these strengths to move forward. I recognised the times in my past where I was strong and I was able to speak out even though others tried to silence me. It takes strength to speak out when things are not right and to speak up for those who are afraid to speak up.

I am now beginning to look ahead, to set goals and try to adopt a healthier way of life. I now want to help other people who are in similar situations, by setting a goal to train as a mentor and hopefully build upon it. I also have learned not to rush, taking one step at a time makes me closer to my goal than where I was yesterday! GLOW thank you for the opportunity, I have learned and gained so much, it was so worth it!

Step 7

'I am strong'

> 'I like to go out there looking like a strong woman, because I am strong. But I am also a woman who goes through all kinds of problems and highs and lows.'
>
> Katy Perry

What are your personal strengths? This is not something we think about daily and many find difficult to embrace their strengths.

If you have been honest throughout this book, you should be at the point where you are able to recognise your great qualities and strengths. Hopefully by now you have begun to recognise things within yourself, you never knew before or you have forgotten as it has been so internalised due to life circumstances. I want to encourage you at this point to embrace these new discoveries as part of your identity.

You are now going to look deep inside to bring out these strengths and acknowledge how they are a part of who you truly are.

Strengths are personal qualities that come naturally to you and that help you perform to a high standard. They are the characteristics that drive you and bring out your passion. We tend to think of them simply as 'You, at your best!'

You can find a list of strengths on the internet if you are really stuck, to help you get started. Write down as many as you think relate to you, then go through your list again looking over your first session, 'I am Valuable' and compare what strengths stand out from this list. Take your time and be honest, what comes more natural to you?

There might be some roles you play in life that the qualities needed don't come naturally and you find you have to work harder at this role. That's okay, you're not aiming for perfection, you are just discovering what your natural strengths are and what areas you need to make more effort on, as it doesn't come too easy.

For example, one of my strengths would be; visionary. I can see the big picture, I dream big dreams about GLOW and other areas of my life. I get passionate about the dreams and visions I have and I know I can lead a team to make this happen. This comes naturally to me. But my weakness would be organisation. If you see my work desk, I like to call it; 'Organised Chaos.' Papers and folders lying everywhere, the filing cabinet is a mess, it takes a lot longer to find one file than it should do as I don't organise the system properly. I will start one project and get halfway through then begin another project because I'm just as passionate about the outcome. I need to have people on my team and in my life who have organisational strengths in order for the vision and plan that I have, to come to fruition. So it is just as important to recognise your weaknesses as your strengths.

From your first session, *'I am Valuable'* use your list of roles you play and list those strengths you have within these roles.

Think of:

- What strengths do you recognise in yourself?
- What strengths do others see in you?
- Rate how satisfied you recognise this strength

STRENGTH	DESCRIPTION	RATE 1-10
E.g. Patience	I can listen to people and recognise it can take time for them to change	6
E.g. Persistence	I don't give up if I know its the right thing to do	8
E.g. Integrity	If I say I am going to do something then I will follow through with it	7
E.g. Generous	I like to give financially and my time to others	9

STRENGTH	DESCRIPTION	RATE 1-10

Notes...

Sandy's Story...

Christmas 2016 was when I was at my lowest point. I can't explain how low I was without telling you a very long story, but my children and I were facing being forced out of our family home of 20 years. I had escaped a long abusive marriage with my three youngest children almost two years before that but my ex continued to abuse me through the court system.

Prior to this, I had been a Project Manager in IT, in charge of 30 people. I gave company presentations on a regular basis to 200 people, I travelled the country to meet with clients on almost a weekly basis. I was a confident professional but this 'man' had persuaded me to give up my career and by the time I left him I had been turned into a mouse. I was unable to talk to anyone, scared even to leave the car in the school car park when picking up the kids. I avoided people as I was too scared I'd say something stupid, like I'd been led to believe.

There was an occupation order on the family home which could have made us homeless. I was in utter despair.

That same morning, I emailed Lighthouse, a local charity that supports those affected by suicide, suicidal thoughts and self-harm as I needed urgent mental health support. They phoned me first thing Monday morning and I made my first appointment. I'd never succumbed to counselling before. Their help was fantastic and I'm so thankful they offered that support at that time. It was Lighthouse who told me about a new course starting in their centre and I was offered a space on the programme. I said Yes and I embarked upon my GLOW journey.

The Real Me course was a journey, but a lovely one. Not one where you were forced to disclose everything, only if you felt comfortable to do so. Each week there was a simple activity to do which helped you explore your life so far, your reactions to it and it also helped you to see a way out of your difficulties. It was so logical.

One of the activities that stands out for me the most was '*Glance Back*' session where we spent the morning cutting out pictures from magazines that represented something in our lives to create a timeline. We didn't have to talk but by that stage we were all such a close-knit family we all wanted to share.

There were stories of brothers dying, mothers dying, babies dying, there were also the happy times, children being born, meeting partners, marrying partners. New homes, holidays, friends and family. It put our lives in perspective. Yes there are some sad times, but there were happy times too.

Another activity was '*Strengths Cards*' where we had to choose which strengths stood out for us, and when we'd collected our own and shared them, the others would take turns and add their own lovely thoughts of you. I think this was the day most tears were shed, but they were tears of love.

Once we'd gathered up the strengths and things we were good at, we used these to set out goals for the future, things we'd love to do. This meant that when the course ended we all had a plan for the future and a whole set of new supportive friends. Friends I've kept in touch with on almost a weekly basis ever since.

One of my goals was to volunteer and use my past career

experience to help charitable causes. I'd tried to get back into my career but 12 years out of IT is a long time and no one wanted me. But I found a home in GLOW, helping with grant applications, organising events and interviewing. And I'm now secretary of the GLOW committee.

I love my visits down to GLOW, even if it's just to get my traditional fry!

"Nobody can change their past but I have learned how to cope with what I have been through. I think if you are forgiving then it means you can get through anything. Once you forgive yourself then everything else just gets on with it."

Step 8

'Glance back'

Take a quick glance back over your life. Remember, you have moved on and you have overcome so many circumstances, issues and hardships. Don't dwell on the past, but use these experiences to motivate you to move forward. There are always people and situations in our life who help us or hinder us.

Task

Create a time line from as far back as you can remember. Be creative in these pages or on a large sheet of paper. Before you get creative, answer these questions to help you on what lessons you can learn from your past.

Think...

- What are the events and who are the people that have made you the person you are today?

- What are the lessons you have learned along the way?

- What challenges have made you stronger?

- How have you emerged a stronger person? (if appropriate)

Sarah's Story...

I moved to North Belfast about a year ago. I had used various mental health services and was running out of options when I heard about GLOW. I have suffered serious mental health issues throughout my childhood and at the age of sixteen I had a manic episode and shortly afterwards, I was diagnosed as being bi-polar.

Bi-polar is horrendous, it is very destructive. It can destroy family connections as it creates resentment with the negative attention that you receive. It can alienate you from friends. Whenever you are in the higher bounds of mania there is a lot of paranoia involved. I found it to be very physically debilitating due to the side effects of the medication. It is considerably difficult to maintain consistent friendships and its almost impossible to work.

My diagnosis came in the middle of my GCSE's and my dad's diagnosis with cancer, it was a really hard time. I just suffered crazy amounts of trauma. I was seen by countless counsellors and psychiatrists, I was admitted at times for stays in psychiatric wards. One of these stays lasted for eight months.

I have tried different types of therapy within mental health. I tried music therapy and a range of counselling however, after the age of 25 it is very hard to get any community support. They weren't ongoing or long-term so you could easily fall back into isolation. I didn't have any friendships or didn't have anywhere to go to when I was struggling again. So I was really excited to learn about GLOW as age wasn't an issue.

I was talking to Chara and I was very curious as it was just for women and I liked the idea of the group aspect. The girls in GLOW have all come from different circumstances and experiences but we all have a connection. Even though we haven't personally been through what others have, we all share the pain. When you share that depth of hurt for one another, it takes your eyes off your own situation and that in itself is therapeutic.

The main reason I needed to be at GLOW was my self-esteem was just rock bottom and my self-belief was rock bottom as well. You can have any amount of help, support and goals but if you don't have self belief and self-esteem then it is nearly impossible to achieve stuff.

I was so excited to start GLOW, just excited for the new experiences. I love being outside and doing outdoor activities so I loved all the team-building exercises we did. Visiting the Belfast Activity Centre was just amazing! Any amount of talking and medication can only do so much, you need to be in the middle of it!

Your time is spent with real women with real issues, no matter how hard your life has been, there are still others who have come through more. I feel that I have been through a lot but still I found myself being shocked and saying;"Wow, I can't believe you have been through that." It is truly inspiring, the strength that women have.

Through GLOW I have revisited my youth and explored what it is that I really enjoy. I love dancing but never took it seriously because I didn't have the confidence to. You really need confidence to be able to dance in front of people. It's amazing now, I really feel comfortable now dancing whether people are watching or not. I have learned to be fearless and totally free to express myself.

Through all the years of speaking to psychiatrists, words are just heavy, now I can express myself through movement, not having to speak. That in itself is so empowering and freeing.

What we learned really early on in GLOW was because we were all sharing so deeply, we could be vulnerable with each other. Although the GLOW programme itself does not incorporate faith based practice, it was so encouraging and refreshing and I believe really important that we could all share honestly about our faith. For me this has been ground breaking as every form of support I have received so far has been secular or clinical. My faith is so important to me and is integral to my life. To be free to share my belief as part of my story has been a much more comprehensive way of recovery.

This in turn made it feel like we had all been friends for years. We got to know each other really well in such a short period of time in fact, most girls were saying that they knew each other better than some of their life-long friends!

I had really struggled in the past with being bullied by girls in school so sitting in a room full of women was not the easiest thing for me. Forming friendships with girls was always difficult for me because of the negative experiences I have had. It's hard not to carry those things with you through life.

However GLOW really hit that all on the head as now I have really well formed friendships with other girls. It's proven to me that I am capable of facing my fears and can be myself and be accepted. Being able to dance in front of people shows me that I am not self-conscious any more. Throughout the course, I just learned to break down those walls of protection that I had built up around myself. I let them down at will and there was healing there as I wasn't isolated or alone.

GLOW offers practical, emotional and hands-on support. A very confident process that works every time. Everyone really enjoys it and wants to keep coming. People have seen the change in me.

The process of GLOW means I am now out the other end, walking in freedom and confidence. I am now setting goals which I wouldn't have done before. I never challenged myself as I didn't believe I could. Whereas I know all my goals are achievable now! "The Me I want to be" session helped me to set these goals and to write down practical, achievable goals.

Step 9

'The Me I want to be'

'Be fearless in the
pursuit of what sets
your soul on fire.'

Unknown

Are you ready to start your journey to make those dreams and visions become a reality?

The inspirational C.S. Lewis said...

"reason is the natural organ of truth; but imagination is the organ of meaning. Imagination, producing new metaphors or revivifying old, is not the cause of truth, but its condition."

In other words we cannot change our future if we do not first envision a better one.

Dr Martin Luther King JR had a dream, which helped to create a better, equal and fair world. He envisaged what the world would look like if it was equal for all. This dream took hold of the world and many others helped to make this dream come true.

Take a moment to envision what your 'ideal life' will look like when you are living in your true identity.

- What do you look like?

- What changes have you made to your life?

- What are you doing/working at?

- Who is with you?

_____

_____

- Who are you serving/helping?

_____

_____

- How are you feeling?

_____

_____

Be creative, and make a collage and life map. Use a notice board and cut out magazines, photographs, inspirational quotes. Be specific in every area, how are you going to do this, when are you going to do this, what do you need in order to achieve this?

Notes...

Gemma's Story...

I had a successful career working for a local bank since 2003 but in 2012 I found myself feelng stuck and becoming increasingly unhappy. I had been working as a Facilitator for the bank from 2005-2008 and loved my job but after having my first child I couldn't return to my role part-time and ended up in a role that I didn't enjoy.

We were living in a lovely 4-bedroom house and I knew that I had to keep working in a job that I didn't enjoy because we had a mortgage to pay and I simply couldn't afford to leave. The pressure of work eventually took its toll on me and I was out of work on sick leave for six months in 2012. During my time off sick I heard about a new personal development programme that was running for women, Chara suggested that I joined to see if it would help me and so I signed up for one of the pilot programmes in May 2012. During the five-week programme I was challenged to consider what was important to me and think about ways to deal with the issues that I was facing. The programme helped me to identify the things in my life that were making me unhappy and gave me the confidence to make changes for the better. At the end of the programme I set goals with an action plan for my future and together with my husband made the decision to sell our house and resign from my job. This was one of the scariest decisions I had ever made but I knew that it was the right decision for myself and my family.

In January 2013 we moved to a smaller house and I got a

part-time job doing administration and accounts. I enjoyed the flexibility and reduced working hours but still felt unfulfilled.

I kept thinking about the positive impact that GLOW had on me and decided to start volunteering for the programme. Chara recognised my skills and experience as a facilitator and gave me an opportunity to facilitate my first personal development programme in 2013 - and as they say the rest is history!

I am now one of the main GLOW facilitators and absolutely love my role! I get so much fulfilment and job satisfaction when I see women changing their lives for the better. I love watching the participants help and encourage each other to reach their full potential. GLOW helped me to gain the confidence to change my life and I am privileged that I can now help others to do the same!

"We had one thing in common though, we are all survivors who don't want to be known as victims, we want to be heroines winning battles!"

Step 10

'My Life Purpose'

> *'If you can't figure out your purpose, figure out your passion. For your passion will lead you right into your purpose.'*
>
> Bishop T.D. Jakes

Congratulations on taking this journey of discovering *The Real You*. Now you have taken these steps, you can build on your learning and celebrate your new discoveries.

No more negative talk and negative actions, speak boldly and positively about yourself, allow yourself to make mistakes and learn, allow yourself to be unique and different, allow yourself the time to be filled and re-energised, allow yourself to be around those positive, life-giving people because you are one of them now!

Let's capture your journey to inspire you to continue…

1

Four most important roles I play daily in my life…

_____

_____

_____

2

Four new self-discoveries…

_____

_____

_____

3

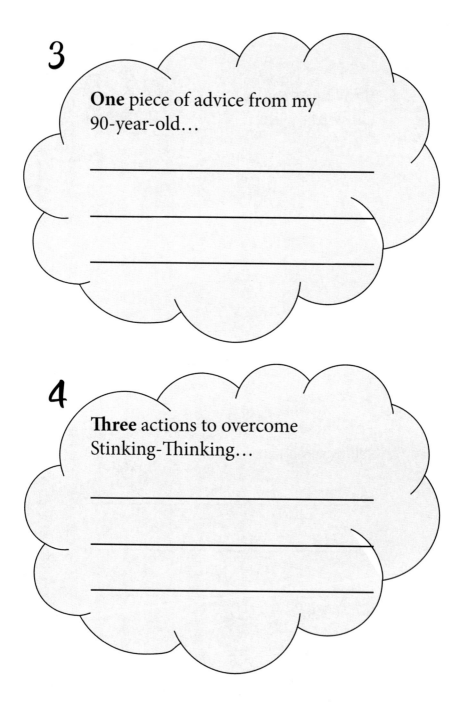

One piece of advice from my
90-year-old…

_____

_____

_____

4

Three actions to overcome
Stinking-Thinking…

_____

_____

_____

5

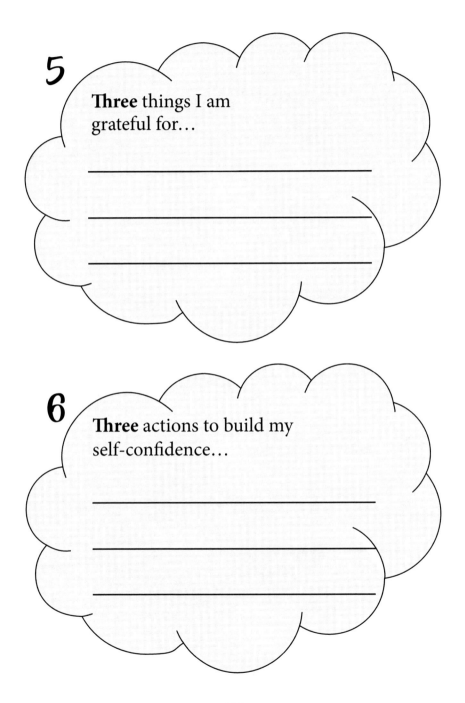

Three things I am
grateful for...

_____

_____

_____

6

Three actions to build my
self-confidence...

_____

_____

_____

7

My top three strengths...

_____

_____

_____

8

One life lesson on
glancing back…

_____

_____

_____

9

One realistic life goal...

_____

_____

_____

10

Three people who will
support me...

_____

_____

_____

Conclusion

"**GLOW** makes you **GLOW**"

Welcome to your GLOW review. Reading this book is only a part of your journey, it's a step in the right direction. I am so proud of you for taking this step and joining with the other hundreds of GLOW women who have also taken action and have set out to discover their true identity.

As you can see, from reading this book, that ACTION is the real verb. I don't believe it's as easy as meditating on good thoughts and the universe will make things happen for you. I do believe it starts with a thought but if it doesn't lead to action then absolutely NOTHING will change and your thoughts will turn to negative thoughts anyway.

One of the major factors of this programme showing results is the support from other women. The friendships and trust that develop because of one main commonality - Change. These women were at a place in life where they were determined to change their circumstances. It was the support from one another that pushed them onto the next step, then the next and so on.

So are you at the point of change after reading this book? Are you ready to take action? Do you want other women to experience the same positive outcomes as you have and as these other women featured in this book have?

Let us help you establish your own GLOW group. Equip other women to GLOW and walk in their true identity.

A GLOW group can take place anywhere you want; your local church women's group, the local community centre, your home or a coffee shop. It can be with women you already have a bond with or you can invite other women to join your group as you begin to meet new women who will bring their uniqueness to the group. And don't forget the tea and cake!

We want to equip you to become a GLOW leader and empower other women to make changes, discover their true identity and live a purpose-filled life. Imagine how you will feel knowing you have been a part of empowering someone to believe in themselves and become the woman she was meant to be. I know that at times when I look at the life-changing circumstances in many women's lives who have come through our programmes, I am overwhelmed. Many women have said it has been life saving! Is this something you want to be a part of?

Please visit our website **www.GLOWni.com** and register your interest in becoming a GLOW leader. We will contact you about our upcoming facilitator training packs.

About Chara...

Chara Clarke is married to Les and has two children Jackson & Cassia and they live in Belfast, Northern Ireland. Chara is a certified Life Coach and is the founder and Manager of **GLOW – Giving Life Opportunities to Women**. Chara is an inspirational women's ministry speaker and loves to stand in front of a group of women to encourage, motivate and inspire them to become all they have been created to be.

Connect with Chara and the GLOW team:

www.GLOWni.com

Would you like to help more women?

Become a facilitator for GLOW!

To register interest visit

www.GLOWni.COM

INSPIRED TO WRITE A BOOK?

Contact Maurice Wylie Media

Inspirational Christian Publisher

Based in Northern Ireland and distributing across the world

www.MauriceWylieMedia.com